The Elements of Management

H. W. Lam, Steven, Faim (Australia)

Copyright © 2012 H.W. Lam, Steven, Faim (Australia)
All rights reserved.

ISBN: 1-4800-6956-6
ISBN-13: 9781480069565

BACKGROUND OF AUTHOR

In the year of 1989, I was then the general manager of a large manufacturing plant, having 118 employees, producing vitreous China sanitarywares in Singapore. The company was then in red and by 1990, I have revamped / restructured the whole company in all aspects of operations and have successfully made the company turned around with a fortune of million dollars of profit by 1991.

In the year of 1992, I was officially appointed as "Director-General (Asia-Pacific / Far East)" by the Russian Government and have incorporated a representative office in Singapore by name of " The Representative Office of the Innovation Fund of the Russian Government." As working "Director-General", I was commercially involved in making arrangement for regional investors to visit Russia to consider investment / joint-venture projects on a two-ways basis. Trading, technologies transfer and pivatization of Russian government projects were also on my priority list. I have traveled extensively to Russia mainly to develop business in Moscow and other cities like St. Petersburg, Siberia, Tatarstan and Uzbekistan for business negotiation / management with or without business groups / tours

Having spent 5 years' time since 1997 in China, I have finally managed to secure the approval of a permit / license to start an education center in the Guangdong province, Jiangmen. The successful experience that I have had been through the total process in securing the final approval was valuable in respect to the knowledge to understand the policies, procedures and other useful requirements in China.

Through thick and thin situation, I have seen China better today in respect to business prospect / opportunity, but however, one must handle situ-

H.W. Lam, Steven, Faim (Australia)

ation with extremely care especially with private parties; and one must also be able to decide the right timing for high profile / publicity in China through the correct mixing around with the right partners and / or associate/s.

THE ELEMENTS OF MANAGEMENT

Q: WHAT IS REAL MANAGEMENT ?

A: YOU MAY FIND YOUR SOLUTION INSIDE THIS BOOK

Q: HOW TO DEFINE TALENT?

A: YOU MAY ALSO FIND YOUR SOLUTION INSIDE THIS BOOK

**: THE STRENGTH OF CHINESE PHILOSOPHIES

1.- GOLD) *WEATHER (TIMING)
2.- WOOD)
3.- FIRE) * LAND / HISTORY (KNOWLEDGE)
4.- WATER)
5.- EARTH) * PEOPLE SUPPORT / PEACE (CREATION)

* THE ABOVE COUNTS IN THE SUCCESS OF MANAGEMENT

AUTHOR :

W.H. LAM, STEVEN, M.Sc.(UK), FAIM (Australia), MASME(USA).

FIRST EDITION

CONTENTS :

1). PEOPLE MANAGEMENT — 1

2). INFRASTRUCTURE MANAGEMENT — 5

3). FOUNDATION OF MANAGEMENT — 9

4). TACTICAL / STRATEGIC MANAGEMENT — 13

5). WORKS MANAGEMENT — 19

6). GLOBAL MANAGEMENT — 25

7). THE LIFESTYLE OF MANAGEMENT — 29

8). THE SECRET OF MANAGEMENT — 33

9). THE DANGER OF MANAGEMENT — 37

MESSAGE

THIS BOOK IS DESIGNED FOR YOUNG EXECUTTVES AND MANAGERS WHO WISH TO ADVANCE THEIR KNOWLEDGE IN RESPECT TO THE MANAGEMENT IN SEQUENCE THAT MAY EMPOWER THEMSELVES TO DEFINE AND OVERCOME PROBLEMS OF FUNCTIONAL ASSIGNMENT BEINGEXECUTED WITH MINIMUM TRIAL AND ERROR.

THE DIRECTION AND INTERPRETATION OF SOLUTION / INFORMATION GWEN IN THIS BOOK VARIED BY THE CATEGORIES OF READERS IN VTEWING AT THE ANGLES THAT THEY FORESEE FROM THEIR READING BY THEIR OWN JUDGEMENT, BACKGROUND AND EXPERIENCE. IF IS A DEFINITE GAIN IN GENERAL BY MOST READERS AFTER COMPLETION OF READING THIS BOOK INDEPTH.

ANSWER.
=========

REAL MANAGEMENT IS AN ABSTRACT TECHNIQUE BEING PRECISELY CULTTVATED WITH AN IN-BORN TALENT BY NATURE TO INFLUENT THE DIRECTION, AFTER RISK CALCULATION WITH CUSHIONING ALLOWANCE, TOWARDS AN EXPECTED BOTTOM-LINE FOR GAIN / PROFIT, IRREGARDLESS OF ANY NEGATIVE OR LINFORESEEN CIRCUMSTANCES THAT MUST BE POSITTVELY TURNAROLIND OR ADJUSTED ACCORDINGLY BASING ON A HANDFUL OF GIVEN SUFFICIENT RESOURCES SUPPORT.

H.W. Lam, Steven, Faim (Australia)

ANSWER

Talent is defined as a special form of brainpower of an individual that can command easily the respects of others plus their full loyalties as well as the possibility to overrule others to work positively in favor to the direction of the expected bottom lines.

One must be a proven top talent professional himself / herself before he or she is eligible to recruit / identify talent of others, otherwise, it is just an empty talk.

1. PEOPLE MANAGEMENT.

This is the most important front line management and it is classified the most vital point of management as it is involved the movement of people in multiple angles. A wrong move will jeopardize eventually the expected bottom line.

(i). EXECUTIVE SEARCH
========================

This involved head hunting, recruitment, interview and selection activities. The pre-selection process involved the basic direction towards the preference of personnel (male / female) to be fitted into :

- What assignment?
- What degree of responsibility?
- What daily working environment involving?
- What category of his / her immediate superior (for daily reporting)?

The selection process involved the next direction of communication and evaluation of the preferred personnel short-listed for the next final round that has / have to be decided/accepted by his / her immediate superior/s. The communication / evaluation of the preferred personnel will be basically angled at:

- The possession of expected qualities and potential to grow.
- Degree of flexibility and know-how to balance / prioritize his / her delegation of responsibility / work flow.

H. W. Lam, Steven, Faim (Australia)

(ii). HUMAN PSYCHOLOGY.

The application of psychology effect is an abstract brainpower / signal to visualize / sense one's action and personalities. It is a mental to mental game. The human mentality is varied from one person to another person; and it maybe define by one's intelligence. (IQ)

(iii). TRAINING & EDUCATION.

The provision of training and education gave good foundation and taught also the art of understanding literally for the people. Methods of training and education play also an important role to cultivate the people to learn / live better. Training differs from teaching as a profession. To some extent, talent maybe cultivate with the help of proper training / education creates miracles education / training received from only real education / teaching respectively.

(iv). EXPERIENCE & DEVELOPMENT.

Experience is a form of practice gained from trial and error; and eventually, one can be developed / upgraded to a higher level / status of professionalism. To some extent, professional talent maybe develop with the support of international experience / exposure from international markets.

The Elements of Management

*Please note and understanding the following flow chart.

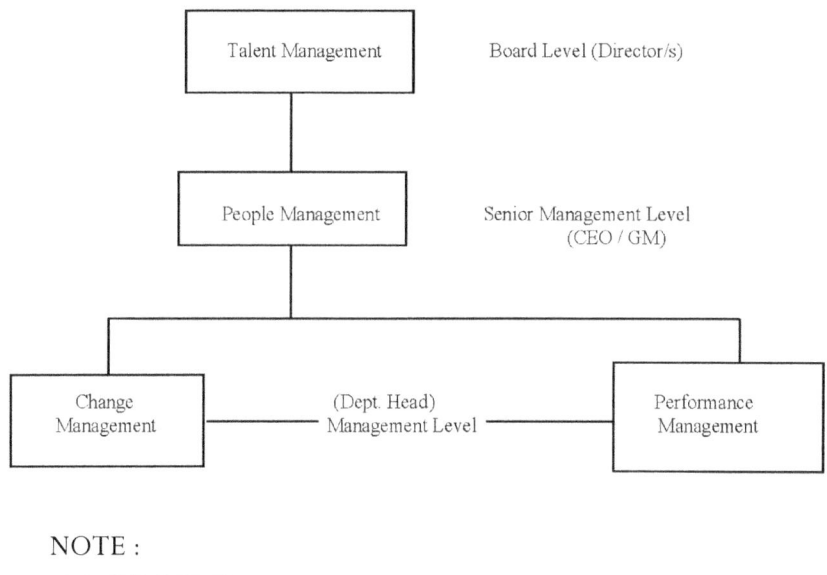

NOTE :
=========

To succeed in people management, one must first succeed in both change and performance management that integrated with an understanding of the balancing of management in principle.

A). Performance Management.
=====================

To establish one's direction of thinking towards :

1). Status.

2). Goal / Ambition.

3). Achievement (in line with proven results).

4). Reward (In line with balancing of work contribution)

H.W. Lam, Steven, Faim (Australia)

Through linking periodically with :

1). Evaluation

2). Analysis

3). Monitoring

4). Fairness

5). Comparison

B).Change Management.
==================

To control one's mind in our favor that situation / environment change in line with our expected bottom line/s with a positive turnaround of one's aptitude and is productivity. The constructive ability to see / absorb one's brain power / thinking in our favor absolutely and positively.

NOTE :
========
A top talented professional in people management classified that he has the constructive ability to identify, recruit, assign and reward fairly in general.

2. Infrastructure Management.

Establishment / Creation of the Infrastructure :

Despite whether a new or existing enterprise / project, the importance of a successful control / establishment of needed personnel as well as a refined delegation / revamp of individual responsibility must be made out clearly and accordingly. The movement of personnel / reporting system must also be spelt accordingly to an organization chart drawn out. The overall infrastructure will be controlled / monitored under the direction of proper personnel that will move the company business overall to achieve a greater height and an expected bottom line depending partly in its implemented infrastructure.

Every company's infrastructure has different angle/s of direction and resources. In view of the said differences, there should be basic involvement of multiple risk calculation related to :

1). Marketing / Timing of Investment.

2). Limitation of returns / profits varied over a timeframe in respect to operational forecasting of its infrastructure.

3). Types of real leadership / entrepreneurship when the infrastructure is well-established it is basically like a good housekeeping or an in-house cleaned up.

H.W. Lam, Steven, Faim (Australia)

Establishment of time factors involving sophisticated know-how to inspire / create by the professionals who used time as a tool to succeed their objectives/s, for instance, time will tell everything under a time table / schedule.

THE MANAGEMENT OF FENGSHUI.
==================================

According to the old Chinese saying, all people born under the following one return cycle :

1). GOLD (metal).
2). WOOD
3). FIRE
4). WATER
5). EARTH
6). Then, back to GOLD (metal) and repeat the cycle 1 to 5.

We must note that no matter how best a professional management expert, he or she is still a human being that can be uncontrollable (beyond his or her limit of will power), as such, luck plays a part to boost up psychologically the morale to increase / achieve one's self-confidence.

Under the one return cycle, one who knows his or her horoscope as a basic guidance / awareness, as such, adjustment can be arranged / made in advance if necessary.

Under the Chinese philosophies spelt also the following three keyed factors :

1). WEATHER - The right timing / opportunity that strikes and grabs it timely.

2). LAND / HISTORY - The indepth knowledge of people, market, product and service

3). People support / peace – The positive creation by / thru peace and support of people and teamwork.

The abovesaid count very much in achieving the success of business management

Formula : Timing + Knowledge + Creation = SUCCESS.

The percentage of success is depending on the degree of positive achievement for each keyed factor.

3. The Foundation of Management :

To create / manage an environment having joy / fun as a value-added to achieve better productivity / goal achievement.

Definition :

Business starts to take place when a customer uses the product / service.

Successful business starts to take place when a customer enjoys using the product / service.

Fun gives natural commitment and intensity ; and the mighty strength of natural commitment and intensity will give a firm direction of focus which will lead to a very high degree of success / achievement. As such, positive solution will be created to overcome problems / obstacles of the majority.

Technique of Fun Management.
==========================

Having fun in business creates good morale for boosting of enthusiasm and psychological effect to upgrade the overall to a higher profile and better productivity in respect to customer service. That will lead to success in making money as a first step.

At this point of time, there must be a limit to it. Not to overjoy in business and forget / relax to strive further to maintain / improve its business is

H.W. Lam, Steven, Faim (Australia)

a danger. As such, we must weigh the consequence – fun of making money is more important or fun of doing business is more important. One who will make no money or less money if he / she considers fun of doing business is more important than fun of making money. Once the thinking is set towards making money is most important as a top priority, then one should consider to make most money in business. Fun creates personal interest.

Self-motivated professionals should understand thoroughly the abovesaid before any implementation should take place in order to avoid self-trapped in an unbalance situation.

THE BALANCING OF MANAGEMENT.

It is quality mixture of right ingredients under a special formulation. The effect of consultancy from an individual professional depending on the right amount of knowledge, training, cultivation, development, education (theory), environmental exposure and working experience (practice through trial and error) as key factors in order to work as real mentor / consultant level. The above said components of assets can only be upgraded periodically as and when opportunity is available to the individual who must preferably have the backup by international exposure in order to derive him or her at the level of talented category with real recognition in a sensitive issue because this may cause discrimination to other qualification provider/s that may not be popular / recognized, but however, its qualification also served well the purpose thoroughly.

In many cases, human being is the first priority as for the qualification of whether recognized or not, it has to be compromised with other ingredients in order to make it a total success. Time is a crucial factor, for example, fruits cannot be eaten when they are unripe. In order to consult one must have absolutely sufficient resources background and knowledge to carry out the consultancy works in a right manner effectively.

The Elements of Management

The technique of management lies on how to balance management with professional ethics. How to balance management in principle both theory and practice ?

The technique involved organization and method linked to time, motion and work study, in addition to related psychology study – behavior, character, personality, etc… The power / talent of listening and analysis is of paramount importance. It is basically quite similar to a production line balancing to ensure the overall management of a company business involving right from the beginning input before the beginning input, the process in operation plus the final output. Good balancing of management is a well-balanced and healthy business diet.

The games of management is an art that controls and leads people to make instruction carefully / accordingly from their leaders to meet up with the required bottom lines which can be good or bad ; and it angle / direction of process can differ depending on how best the games are played by the leaders / operators.

To get the best results, one must know how to absorb, defend and attack under the right position / timing. One must also know his surrounding infrastructure and people well in order to gain the piece of mind to work / think calmly and productively.

The games of management can play wonders and its unique part is endless whether success and/or failure. Do not worry of failure, it may make you a stronger, happier and healthier person. Failure possibly cultivates a person to enjoy success after failure.

The management of conflict / argument depending on the management of personality / psychology that give achievement of the final management goal involving the technique of listening, expression and observation.

H.W. Lam, Steven, Faim (Australia)

The power of management has enlightened us its strength being transferred and changed situations having entangled problems to achievement of solutions in final. The mentality of management has its strength to cultivate / nourish though that gives the individual a chance to acquire so-called "Mentality Technique" which one can overcome criticism from others. When one's mentality is stable and calm, the power of management increases positively in order to achieve the success and reality of management.

4.
Tactical / Strategic Management.

In order to manage well, one requires to establish his or her strategies basically in the following angles :

1). Strategy Research and Analysis.
==============================
Manage to collect and analyse accurate / relevant datas for further review and refinement purpose.

2). Planning Strategy.
====================
Formulate and evaluate business plans or work plans according to the existing / available resources.

3). Operational Strategy.
=====================
Activate and monitor plans while in action ; and adjust as and when required.

4). Tactical Strategy.
=====================
After refinement, an advance tactic / technique has been developed to ensure better / expected results.

H.W. Lam, Steven, Faim (Australia)

The effect of strategy is strengthen in line with the right tactic applied according to the given working atmosphere, available resources (assets / manpower) and market environment / condition.

Case Study 1.
============

Title : The Rise and Fall of a business investment / venture in China.
===

The following basic key factors / issues in sequence are highlighted in general worth consideration.

1). To understand the basic needs, regulations, formalities and groundworks (eg. approval application, pre-arrangement, preparation, etc...)

2). To understand the intermediate level of policies, needs and its groundworks. (eg. processing time, downtime, etc..)

3). To understand the higher intermediate level of terms and conditions (eg. Approval, trial run period, etc..)

4). To understand the advanced level of criteria (eg. new policies (internal and external) to overrule old policies even after approval, etc..).

5). To understand finally the local human mentality / customary (their local ways of doing business)

6). To understand the infrastructure / environment of China since China has indeed many years of history, as such, the practice of business must comply hand-in-hand accordingly to their lifestyle and circles of games.

7). To understand and comply timely to their general policies periodically, as such, one must know how to prepare ahead before new policies implementation will be beneficial for business purpose. There are plenty rooms of opportunites for people to succeed and fail in their business with no fixed timeframe.

8). To understand timely the financial aspects periodically in order to upgrade one's knowledge in the financial / banking circles. This will be a value-added to one's business gain indefinitely.

9). To understand and able to work closely hand-in-hand with the relevant levels of authorities preferably at the first priority of ranking as follow :

1). Central government
2). Provincial government.
3). City government.
4). County government.
The following causes failure of management :

1). Mismanagement–Poor leadership, poor system, poor planning, etc..

2). Miscalculation–lack of precise market research / knowledge, unforseen risk, etc..)

3). Wrong projection–Inaccurate forecast / realization, unrealistic goal and its limit.

4). Wrong Timing–Unknown maturity period.

5). Wrong perception–Creation of misunderstandings.

6). Human Psychology–Lack of good human rapport / relationship, wrong thinking, wrong expression and wrong judgement.

H.W. Lam, Steven, Faim (Australia)

Case Study 2.

Types of Bank Instrument :

Commonly used bank instrument in the commercial / financial circle are :

1). Banker's Guarantee (BG).

It is an irrevocable letter of guarantee issues from a bank and it maybe use in the following manners :

i. To act as a security deposit for / on behalf of an individual or company.

ii. To use as a collateral pledge against the funding bank for the purpose of supporting projects funding.

Terms and conditions of the BG verbiage will be spelt / issued by the receiving bank, but however, the issuing bank must also be willing to accept / agree to the BG verbiage from the receiving bank. It works two-ways.

2). Standby Letter of Credit (SBLC).

It is an irrevocable bank instrument issues from a bank and it maybe use in the following manner :

To use as a collateral pledge against the funding bank for a loan / credit line in support of projects funding purpose and the normal maturity period is one year one day in general for SBLC under the ICC 600, mode of transaction is by S.W.I.F.T. bank to bank.

3). Commercial Letter of Credit.
===========================

It is an irrevocable bank instrument issues from a bank and it maybe use in the following manner :

i. Irrevocable letter of credit at sight issues for trade purpose involving shipment of goods/cargoes as a form of secured payment term between the seller and buyer. Trade letter of credit protects agreed terms and conditions to some extent between the seller and the buyer basing on the following details :

Shipment of goods / cargoes : departure / arrival dates - port of discharge on F.O.B. or C.I.F. basis. F.O.B. is freight on board of the country of the exporter / seller and C.I.F. isthe country of the importer / buyer. Clarification must be cleared on this issue.

5. Works Management.

To manage works flow, different categories of works study involved in respect to the following areas :

i. BUSINESS :
=======================

To manage a business, a basic combination of knowledge, exposure, practice, confidence and business acumen.

ii. FACTORY :
=========================

To manage a factory, proper allocation and full use of available resources given in respect to manpower, materials and machinery as well as industrial relations applicable.

iii. ENGINEERING :
===========================

This function is to target at plant maintenance / repair in respect to give support to factory a building as a technical back-up / requirement.

iv. INFORMATION TECHNOLOGY :
=================================

This function is integrated to all functions / departments within enterprise / organization. internet through computers can be used in/out of the company from the service point of view. Effective information and communication can be stored and activated within finger tips at speed.

v. FINANCE / ACCOUNTS :

This function is inter-linked with auditing, accounting and most importantly, precise cashflow projection must be prepared on the basis of short, medium and long term – weekly, monthly and quarterly respectively.

vi. LOGISTICS :

This function covers basically inventory control, transportation, warehousing and purchasing. It can be a tool in form of professional service globally. The power of logistic gives the main benefits of lost saving and efficiency.

vii. ADMINISTRATION / PERSONNEL :

This function is to organize / manage the operations that one must prepare to overcome sensitive issues like :

- Reshuffle of personnel / manpower.
- Reinforce / enforce new work systems and policies in the company.
- To decide/review the performance / growth of personnel.
- To implement training programs as and when requires as to upgrade the efficiency of manpower.
- To conduct interview, selection and recruitment of personnel.

One must also be administratively excellent/talented in order to put the whole enterprise healthy by basic means of :

- Identifying and understanding the whole administrative system in the company thoroughly / rightly in order to adjust progressively the unproductive habits.
- The ability to communicate, lead, motivate and interact with people of all levels.
- To gain respect from all levels of personnel.

Proper administration is like a vital point of a human being that can cause disruption to other systems / functions which can bring down the overall working morale of personnel thereby affecting the working environment inclusive of the productive direction. One must not underestimate this important function and not to forget the proper leadership qualities as a combination are also very useful as a whole.

Consolidation of personnel is of paramount importance because its cohesive strength manage to meet / achieve maximum results with a common interest of all. In order to exercise effectively in manpower management, one must be a better leader to see work problems in order to organize / manage a good team. In order to manage or select a talent professional, one must first be a top talent himself / herself before he or she be able to overcome / gain the true respect from his / her subordinate/s or the talent professional/s.

NOTE :
========

Factory operations involved the following functions in sequence :

1). Manpower.
==============

Planning of Manpower

Organizing, Charting of Manpower.

Allocation of Manpower.

H.W. Lam, Steven, Faim (Australia)

Manpower Analysis and Research.

Monitoring of Manpower.

2). Materials / Machinery.
========================

Materials Planning and Control.

Monitor / Analyze Materials Flow and Usage.

Machinery Maintenance/Repair Schedule.

Materials / Parts Ordering and Stock Planning including Ordering Schedule.

3). Production.
===============

Production Planning and Control.

Production Schedule inter-linked with the daily sales schedule.

Master Production Schedule.

The below chart has shown works study can be broken into two (2) categories - Time Study and Motion Study applicable for factory/manufacturing operations ; and Organization and Method applicable for office operations. In order to conduct works study, involvement of time study plus motion study at the same time, formula :

Measure Time + Motion = Works Study.

The Elements of Management

To complete a job or business or production, for example, we count the time for action / movement taken and instantly, we should shortlist also the preferable movement / action taken at the shortest possible time. Works Study will upgrade productivity. It pays profit

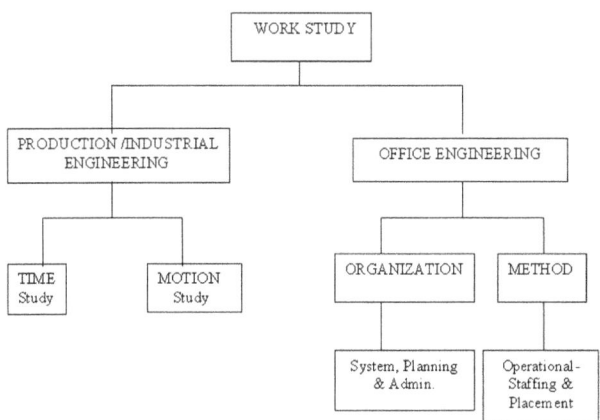

6.
Business Management (Global).

To start an overseas business :

In order to start and run smoothly a business venture successfully whether in China, Russia, Vietnam, etc... one must have the following assets / qualities :

1). PERSONAL RAPPORT.
=========================

Strong business connection and people relationship will give strength to the foreign party (eg. investor) so that the party can activate smoother with much less obstacles / problems.

2). LANGUAGES.
==================

Able to communicate and read the respective language and this will definitely be an asset so that to minimize any misunderstandings including dialogue with familiar frequency, as such, this will bring the two parties (foreign and local) much closer with fuller trust quite like blood brothers in one family.

H.W. Lam, Steven, Faim (Australia)

3). PERSONAL SACRIFICATION.
===============================

One must have the guts and willingness to sacrifice his / her personal time according to the requirement of the respective country ; and as far as investment is concerned, one must also be smart enough to spend / pay in a flexible manner, but bearing in mind towards achievement of the bottom lines.

In order to have a good grasp of the global management, one must expose to much business travel extensively within the regional / international markets and must also involve practically the transaction of business in various forms related to import, export, trading, marketing and investment / joint-venture. Eventually, time will try to strengthen one's background in business development / acumen..

Below are some basic general details concerning various countries and it maybe useful as a guide for new business travelers for the first time abroad.

i.) RUSSIA.
==========

Western – related food. Religion : Christianity. Historical environment. Capital : Moscow. These are loyalists committed in the technical / commercial sectors ; and Russians learn very quickly. English language is getting popular in Russia amongst the younger generation. Business can be developed especially the trust is being built with the Russians. Market potential is very good towards property, trading, shipping, comodities, etc ...

ii.) CHINA.
============

Chinese – related food. Religion : Free thinker or Buddism. Historical environment. Chinese / Mandarin is the main language in the country. The system / policy in the country still being overruled to some extent in all aspects of businesses, therefore, causing the process much lengthy and complicated.

Oversea investors find difficult to understand / see the clear cut business direction in the long run, except short term basis around one year timeframe. Market potential is good towards logistic, food, property, education & training, etc...

iii.) HONG KONG.
=================

Main dialect / language : Cantonese / Chinese . Popular Cantonese food. Availability :

Human rights, freedom of speech. It is a popular business and financial center. Fast pace of business development. It is a good stop point / transaction point for the assessment to China business market which is nearby to Hong Kong. In the past, it is governed under the United Kingdom and its legal systems are British-related. Hong Kong has today seven million in population with a modern lifestyle and good infrastructure which is beneficial for various industries, eg entertainment, food, shipping, etc.. Market potential is good towards property, trading, stock, food, financial, etc...

iv.) Southeast Asia.
==================

Asia region comprises of five countries – Singapore, Malaysia, Indonesia, Thailand and Philippines ; and Southeast Asia has mighty resources such as timber, rice, sugar, palm oil, latex / rubber, seafood, etc… Of all the five countries, Singapore will stand as the most developed country classified as the well-known regional hub for shipping and oil refinery. Singapore has its port facilities and respected name for its greenery and cleanliness of its city with good infrastructure overall and telecommunication facilities being created to serve the people to live in a safe and sound environment towards high technologies and industralization. Market potential : Fantastic in general. Singapore, a rich country, has good management habits in track record, as such, good image will attract more investors and industrialists.

H.W. Lam, Steven, Faim (Australia)

v.) INDIA.

India has a tremendous network of business link to trade and other forms of business cooperation with other countries worldwide, especially Asia-Pacific region and Russia. India has great resources and has its unique cultures. Most Indians understand English language and the market potential is very good towards textile, garment, property, granite, marble, diamonds, gold, tea, coffee, seafood, etc...

NOTE :
=========

Beside the technical experience gained from overseas exposure, one must master the art of relationship ; and as a matter of fact, one must also be prepared to sacrifice to some extent personally. To capture the overseas commercial market or to overturn one's thinking, the seller has to be sincerely and emotionally expressed the calculated facts and true feelings towards the direction of all parties' benefits for good.

7. The lifestyle of Management.

Every human beings has different lifestyle in their family brought up, training background, works exposure, etc… and all these eventually will give different types of motivation and development of personality as well as one's mentality.

Every human beings has different strength of management in view of non-comparable personal qualities of every individual that has different power of understanding, background, knowledge and interpretation.

In view of the long and short points of every human beings is having, it is also known as the plus point and the minus point, as such, the application of management become inaccurate, therefore, it cannot be precisely implemented, eg. policies, systems, plans, action, etc…

The failure and success of management depend partly on the firmness / precision of the action taken and/or details transferred (eg. direct or indirect) from one place to another.
In order to minimize failure, there must be a certain degree of tolerance, refinement and flexibility to such action (management decision) taken for any transaction / project.

The lifestyle of human beings fall under different categories of persons who can manage differently at their own styles of management under their responsibilities / assignment given right down by the board of directors.

H.W. Lam, Steven, Faim (Australia)

Majority of the seasoned working professionals are talented whether they are academically talented or practically talented ; and such personality value is classified as "Talent".

Talent is basically defined by evaluating one's six / common sense, precise thinking and able to sense / see through crucial happening / things in ahead that can or cannot give excellent returns / results eventually after its course of action within a time frame.

The complexity of management involved both healthy and unhealthy lifestyles of leadership due to that in order to adapt oneself to the given environment for the purpose of achievement despite going against own principles. A high degree of initiative requires to breakthrough the layer of obstacles in order to have the free hands to manage the patterns expected as per bottom line/s.

THE BASIC UNDERSTANDING OF BANK INSTRUMENT.
==

In the financial circle, the basic knowledge is required for the following investment / commercial involvement :

1). Bank Guarantee (BG).
=========================

It is a letter of guarantee from a bank issued by either a local or foreign bank directly to another funding bank that receive it and it maybe use as a collateral pledged to the funding bank that finally provides projects funding to the beneficiary who is a current client of the funding bank. There is a maturity / expiry date on the bank guarantee depending on the project period.

2). Standby Letter of Credit. (SBLC).
=====================================

It operates quite similar to the abovesaid bank instrument and the expiry period is normally one year from the date of issue from the issuing local or foreign bank. Its format to follow the ICC600 in general.

NOTE :
========

In order to activate the abovesaid instrument, the funding bank must first to be agreed to support his customer and agreed also to accept the issuing bank ; and its verbiage of SBLC or BG preferably come from the funding bank is preferable.

Commercial Letter of Credit.
========================

It is strictly used for trading, import and export of goods transaction between the seller and the buyer. this bank instrument will normally compromise with shipment document like packing list, proforma invoice, insurance, certificate of origin (optional), etc…

Depending on whether C.I.F. (cost insurance and freight) or F.O.B. (freight on board) for which country ? One must ensure that the full description / contents of the terms and conditions stated on the commercial letter of credit must tally with all document like the proforma invoice, etc…

8. The Secrets of Management.

At the level of general management, one should have been through stages of training, education and experience involvement as mentioned under the contents of this book, from basic management of human beings until the lifestyle of management. After all these hardship, to some extent, one has mastered/understood the secrets of management which maybe defined as the reality of management.

How to identify / interpret the reality of management ? One has been through many years of trial and errors in his / her management career, from thereon, one has really learnt the hard /complicated ways to problems solving and has also the ability to produce solutions, the individual may value / limit such achievement of success as secrets, but such confidential details are the reality to management success.

The successful history of an individual may not be applicable to another party / individual in respect to basically due to different family brought up, personality, education, training, timing, experience, environment, availability/ types of resources, exposure and other qualities ; and normally, such success history cannot be accurately elaborated / transferred and/or applicable to other individual/s.

It is a good thing for an engineer to be specialized in a subject like mechanical or production or electrical, but as for a departmental manager, he or she may specialize in managing a department like marketing or finance or logistic, however, it is also a good thing to expose the departmental manager to other working areas. An all-rounded management experience / exposure gives an individual the strength (value-added) to understand and carry out his or her given assignment in a more diplomatic manner. Technically, one has to be firmed and specialized is necessary, but administratively, there must be a certain allowance ready for the flexibility / cushioning and interchange as and when necessary for the purpose of achievement in respect to interpersonal and smooth communication.

The prospect of management career, one must be able to see the rare potential of widening his or her horizon / future that can give him/her the better opportunity to capture / fulfill his or her ambition in the shortest period especially the unique and rich experience that can be achieved abroad (regional / international). An international traveler sees things better and wider angle than one has not been traveling abroad in his or her lifetime.

The core of management can be value-added by means of true power of brainstorming in exchange of ideas that will turn around into positive/constructive action. To achieve this exercise, a team spirit is required to support / share its achievement / failure.

The silence of management is like the old saying "Clear Water Run Deep". The secret of management lies in the depth of management like a Indonesia/Malay language called "Kueh Lapis" which consisting of several layers after layers. The patterns of management is defined as follows :

1). The outer layer—This category defines the basic problems used to happen in a daily management function.

2). The inner layer—This level defines the secondary problems rarely happen to be solved under the senior management.

3). The final layer—This stage defines the most complicated problems rarely to happen that must be solved under the direction of the top management / board of directors.

THE BRAINPOWER OF MANAGEMENT.

The hidden treasure of management is defined like a human brain that challenge, tackle and stabilize all problems created and eventually with solutions return in favor of the management expert / provider in final as a bottom line.

NOTE :

Further than this final layer, external professionals or exceptionally the solution providers maybe selected / requested to provide the right answer/s, but it is a question mark ?

9.
The Danger of Management.

Management is an art and is also a game which can control and lead the organization towards a healthy or unhealthy turnaround of its infrastructure and its bottom line of achievement. Kindly note the following view points of this final episode / topic :

    i.) The technical behavioral aspects of management is a value-added formula / ingredient to its management technique with a touch of humor and its professional ethics that can positively turnaround / heal existing circumstances / problems respectively.

    ii.) The political aspects of management cover the daily involvement of personnel in every organization that creat common power struggle and working differences amongst colleagues.

    iii.) The combination of both aspects of behavior and political practice in management, it gives a total different faces of professional practice / ethic that make management life / career more successful / interesting, but complicating to some extent. In order to achieve, one may have to go against his/her own conscious / will. To misuse proper management practice / ethic, there will be a creation of miscommunication / misunderstanding, time wastage, etc... that affect profit gain and manpower talent. In order to activate management practice, there must first have proper evaluation and analysis by real management professional/s to give the green light. One must know what is real opportunity and how to treasure/define the real opportunity ? If such said opportunity available, one must make full usage as time waits for no men and real opportunity cannot be bought or shared or reversed by any individual.

The proper implementation and discipline of management is governed by its professional ethics (mind and heart) as a success, otherwise, as a reverse, without the self-conscious of activating such said ingredients mixed, the result is to destroy the nice set-up / building just overnight or over a period of time.

Why and how management can be classified under "danger" category which is clarified basically in two forms :

1). To manage without any bad intention / ulterior motives.

As such, to run / manage transparently a business or enterprise with full heart and mind to achieve positively the bottom lines on behalf of the enterprise in the long run without personal gain / interest.

2). To manage with ulterior motives / bad intention.

As such, to run / manage a business or enterprise positively to achieve the bottom lines on behalf of the enterprise with personal gain in time to come. The calculated ingredients of management that can keep the enterprise running to only some extent although the outlook of the bottom lines of the enterprise are achieved. It is a matter of time, a downfall will happen to the enterprise. In order to save / extend it, the same old management team of the enterprise may possibly save / extend it, not a new management team takeover, otherwise, the enterprise will be collapsed in due course unless there is a total revamp.

The change of management is a hidden strategy / technique applicable by the one who first implemented the system/policy and run the show overall, as such, that individual will have the antidote to cure arising problems because that individual has the calculated formula.

How to overcome the danger of management ? The real talent of management can help to resolve / overcome it, but there are many other factors must take into consideration to compromise / support the one who is going to exercise the technique of psychology / people management.

The danger of management inter-linked with the revengeful intention under this category and it will take place to overturn/sabotage the success of management into failure.

In the worst consequence, it is the end of management when one who must have the guts required and must also prepare to die for the worst. Death is the final choice that linked to the game of management involving the gambling of life investment – To live or die !

One of the secrets depends on the technique of human control exercise through the effect of mental psychology relating to the following main factors :

1). Materialistic reward in form of money.
======================================

Take for example, if a person is given a salary of USD1million per year and this person is very obedient to his / her immediate superior as to please his/her boss due to materialistic reward given, but his/her performance wise is just fair. This type of situation is just a temporary measure to look good only over a period of time. It is unhealthy for the boss / investor. This is known as short term planning under the danger of management that can destroy everything over a period of time.

In the long run, will the boss survive / maintain such high salary payment unless there is a windfall / fantastic of income / profit. Each year, the expenditure grows and if the economic situation cannot be controlled, bankruptcy will take place, as such, the style of management effects through monetary rewards and this is known as the game of management. The other problem is that such practice will create a gap between staff of all ranks due to salaries different are great.

H.W. Lam, Steven, Faim (Australia)

For the sake of long term planning, no gimmick, it is proper to do the other way round, that is, salary pays according to the strength of the company as well as its staff on the basis as working employees. The balancing of management must take place commercially to ensure it make sense, otherwise, where the money come from for fat salaries ?

If the fat salaries keep on to grow, there will be a day when the situation will explode and all matters will come to a standstill or collapse. This is known as hit and run management and whosoever takeover the continuation of the business, it is only a final empty shell.

As such, everything has to start all over again from zero. The underhand of management is extremely complicated / dangerous, and it is worse than mismanagement because this category of management could be on purpose intentionally. To control this to happen, someone with real top talent is needed in order to overcome / oversee such danger of management at an early stage. How to define real top talent ? One who must first be a real top talent himself / herself before he / she is qualified to identify, screen and recruit professionals with top talent. He / she cannot identify what is talent if he / she is not a talent professional. A professional with talent is one who will know how to define what is talent and how to appreciate talented professionals, as such, they can get together happily / speaking professionally the same language at the same frequency. This is a very constructive / productive work force as a professional team.

A professional with talent has the following basic qualities :

1). Able to read accurately one's mind and action through one's personality, behavior, character, expression, thought, etc...

2). Able to sense the right timing for presentation / action to be taken in a diplomatic manner that can overcome / gain respect from others.

3). Able to decide the direction of movement, action to be taken and to face the final event irregardless of whatever bottom lines. Be prepared for it !

The Elements of Management

The Downfall of Management categorized as follow :

Firstly, it caused by intentional action with ulterior motives to purposely sabotage with plan/s in advance to pursue the bottom line of purely personal gain / interest.

Secondly, it caused by unintentional action with good motive and to place the interest of all as priority and strive towards the bottom line of achievement above self-interest.

Failure caused by :

i.) Lack of talent, experience, training, common sense (IQ) and exposure in general.

ii.) Lack of personal qualities like determination, judgement, business acumen, leadership, independence, communication, negotiation, etc....

NOTE :
==========

Education plays only one basic part of success and the balance of the other part of success plays depending on the individual case to case as mentioned above.

The category / guidance of management :

One has to climb the management ladder step by step from the status of junior level to senior level. It will cause damage to the management structure if decision made without proper direction from the qualified senior management rank, depending on background.

The collapse of management affecting the management backbone and it starts when minority of the problems unsolved and/or being covered up through making an untrue management report.

H. W. Lam, Steven, Faim (Australia)

SUMMARY.
===============

The technique of mind management is to control one's mind spiritually that can manipulate him or her in favor towards the direction of the mind controller. In order to achieve such technique, one must be a top talent by nature coupled with a series of proper general education, real management, training & education, right working environment / exposure, and cultivated professional discipline. This is the highest level in real management that one can move people at his/her command. alternatively, it is a form of discipline management under this said technique.

In order to reinforce the pillars /circles of management, we must first have real management mentality rightly fixed into whatsoever situation in a flexible /adaptable manner that can turnaround any situation upside down in line with the spelt management objectives.

The management has preliminary introduced and classified as in the market generally a subject involved both theory and practice just before the further the step of real management as a most advance level of sophisticated technique to ensure success and return according to one's wish.

Both theory and practice of management have turned into a powerful technique of real management, the king of management, is like a constructive device that can turnaround all problems into solutions confidently and positively without fail.

Psychology applies to both technique of hard and soft management of disciplines that under the learning process of education, training and development. When psychology applies in a proper manner, the positive effect will be achieved successfully in respect to the required bottom lines expected from all levels of supervisory and managerial ranks.

Having achieved the reality of management will give the power of management basically comprising of successful achievement of the management psychology effect plus the assets (qualities/resources hand) of management that will finally give / achieve the goal set for capital gained in terms of monetary and people management.

The Heart of Real Management is the power of heart technique is between heart to heart of two or more human beings. The application of such technique should apply professionally at the right time, with the right person and with the right presentation having a very flexible mentality approach in a diplomatic manner.

www.ingramcontent.com/pod-product-compliance
Lightning Source LLC
Chambersburg PA
CBHW061519180526
45171CB00001B/248